Edexcel Economics A
Theme 2: The UK economy - Performance and Policies

By

Brendan Case,

Other titles in this series

Edexcel Economics A
Theme 1: Introduction to Markets and Market Failure
Theme 3: Business Behaviour and the Labour Market
Theme 4: A Global Perspective

ISBN 978 1515239024

Table of contents

<u>About the author</u>

The author is Head of Economics at Ashbourne Independent Sixth Form College in London, and is a graduate of the London School of Economics. He has been teaching the Edexcel A level economics syllabus for over 15 years, and has also been an examiner for this syllabus.

Measures of economic performance of countries

1

There are four of these:

- Inflation
- Unemployment
- Balance of payments
- Gross Domestic Product (GDP)

Let's look at these one by one.

Inflation

2

2.1 Definition

Inflation is the persistent tendency of prices to rise.

2.2 Measurement

Inflation is measured using the Consumer Price Index (CPI). It shows the changes in the prices of an average person's shopping basket. It's based on a EU wide formula and so makes the UK rate of inflation directly comparable to other EU countries. The old measure was called the Retail Price Index (RPI), but the CPI replaced that in 2011. The RPI used to be known as the 'headline' rate of inflation. The CPI excludes mortgage interest payments and rent but the RPI includes them.

2.3 Constructing the CPI

(1) Each year a shopping survey is done to determine the most popular items in the average UK shopping basket. This is known as the Living Costs and Food Survey (LCF). It involves collecting information from a sample of approximately 6,000 households who use self-reported diaries to record all purchases, including food eaten out.

(2) The proportion of income spent on each item is recorded and a weight is assigned to each category, e.g. a weight of 350 for food would indicate on average 35% of household income is spent on food. Over 650 items are selected in total and they range from food and clothes to housing and transport.

(3) From this a price index is constructed with a base year starting at 100. Every month the price index is recalculated, by a price survey in shops, and compared to the base, so that the index is a weighted average of price increases not just a straight average of price increases, e.g. if the index increased to 102.5 over the year this would mean that inflation was 2.5% for the year.

2.4 Limitations of the CPI

No person is average – the goods in the 'average shopping basket' will apply to very few people because everybody has different spending patterns. Therefore it may lack accuracy.

Problems in collecting the data – there are always problems collecting the data from the CPI surveys, e.g. recording errors, lack of staff training. This calls into question the reliability of the figures. The response rate to the LCF in 2011 was only 54%.

Changes in the composition – the CPI has to change in composition every year to reflect changes in taste and habit. This means it's never truly comparable over time, e.g. in 2012 tablet computers were added and colour camera film dropped.

Changes in quality, design and performance of products – the CPI only measures changes in price not performance, quality and design. The price of a product may have risen but by comparison these may have risen much faster, e.g. PC's – therefore they won't be reflected in the CPI.

Changes in indirect tax – increases in VAT and customs duty increase the price of goods but they are not true price increases. Therefore this can distort the meaning of the CPI.

Mortgage interest payments – the CPI excludes mortgage interest payments and rent. This means if it is used in wage negotiations wage increases may fail to take into account a large amount of household expenditure.

Regional variations – the CPI is for the whole country but regional variations exist.

2.5 RPI, RPIX and RPIY

RPI – the old way to measure inflation. The main point to remember is that it includes mortgage interest payments and rent but the CPI doesn't.

RPIX - this is the RPI excluding mortgage interest payments. It's to get over the distorting effect that raising interest rates to slow down inflation can have on the RPI. The composition is very similar to the CPI.

RPIY - this is the RPI excluding mortgage interest payments and indirect tax. It's to get over the problems caused by having mortgage interest payments and indirect tax in the RPI.

Unemployment

3

3.1 Unemployment, underemployment, economically inactive

You should be clear about these definitions.

Unemployment - means those people who don't have a job, but have been actively seeking work in the past four weeks and are able to start work in the next two weeks.

Underemployment - means part-time workers who are doing less hours than they want to.

Economically inactive - means those people who don't have a job, but are not actively seeking work, e.g. students, long-term sick, housewives, early retired.

3.2 Ways of measuring unemployment

(i) Claimant count

This is the number of people claiming the job seekers allowance (JSA). The figures are published monthly.

Advantages

- Cheap to collect
- Available every month
- It's a complete count and not a survey

Disadvantages

- It's based on administrative rules – therefore it excludes certain groups, e.g. anyone under 18, people over 60, full time students, the long-term sick and those claiming Incapacity Benefit (IB)
- Provides limited analysis of the characteristics of the unemployed

(ii) Independent Labour Organisation (ILO) Survey

The ILO survey takes its figures from a wider survey of employment called the Labour Force Survey (LFS). The LFS is carried out on a quarterly basis and is done by a telephone survey on about 600,000 households involving 100,000 adults. The survey collects details on household size and composition, age, sex, marital status, ethnic origin and occupation of residents.

Advantages

- It's the internationally recognised way of calculating unemployment – therefore the UK's unemployment rate can be directly compared with other EU countries.
- Provides more detailed characteristics of the unemployed, e.g. occupation, age, gender.

Disadvantages

- More costly to collect
- Figures are only available every quarter
- Prone to sampling and response errors

(iii) Why is the ILO survey figure always above the claimant count figure?

- The claimant count excludes certain groups, e.g. people over 60, everybody under 18.
- Sampling and response errors on the survey.
- Some people may be out of work but not claiming benefit, e.g. stigma attached to claiming it, people may be unemployed for short periods and it's too much trouble to fill in all the forms, tight criteria applied to eligibility.

3.3 Other problems of measuring unemployment

- Part-time workers – measurements of unemployment don't take into account unused resources. Part-time workers are counted as 'employed' not 'part-time unemployed'. In 2012 the working population of the UK was approximately 30m of which about 25% were part-time workers. Of those about 20% (1.5m) would liked to have had a full-time job but couldn't find one.

Balance of payments

4

4.1 Definition

The balance of payments is the sum total of a country's income and expenditure on foreign trade together with all its international capital movements. It's split into two sections - the current account, and the capital and financial account.

4.2 Current account

The current account shows trade in goods and services. It also shows income from employment and investments from abroad and transfers which have been made by governments and individuals. There are two different types of imports/exports – visibles and invisibles.

Visible imports / exports – these are goods that you can see, touch and feel, e.g. cars, manufactured goods, oil.
Invisible imports/ exports – this is trade in services or income and profits from foreign subsidiaries, e.g. insurance, tourism, shipping, profits from foreign subsidiaries, dividends.

When exports are bigger than imports it's called a surplus, when imports are bigger than exports it's called a deficit.

4.3 Capital and financial account

This records capital inflows and outflows. It's made up of three types of transaction – direct capital investment including FDI, portfolio investments in stocks/shares and bonds, and lastly banking flows ("hot money"). The balance on the capital and financial account should be equal and opposite to the current account balance, so the balance of payments always balances. In reality the capital and financial account always contains a 'balancing item' which represents errors or omissions in the figures.

Capital inflow - e.g. a Japanese company investing in a car manufacturing plant in the UK (FDI); a foreign bank making a loan to a UK company.

Capital outflow - e.g. a UK company investing abroad; a UK bank making a loan to a foreign company

4.4 How to know if a transaction is an import/export or capital inflow/ outflow

A lot of the time this is straightforward but if it isn't always look at the direction the money is moving in rather than the goods or services. With exports or capital inflows money is always coming into the country.

Examples

- UK company abroad sending profits or dividends back to the UK = invisible export
- Japanese company sending profit or dividends back to Japan = invisible import
- UK resident abroad sending money back to the UK = invisible export
- Japanese resident in the UK sending money back to Japan = invisible import

4.5 Classifying the exports of foreign companies in the UK

The exports of foreign companies, e.g. Nissan, Toyota from the UK are counted as UK exports and therefore improve the balance of payments. This is one of the reasons why the government is keen to encourage inward foreign investment.

4.6 Other important points

- The balance of trade - this is another name for the current account.
- The visible trade balance is often called the 'balance of payments' by the media – so look out for this in data response questions.

Gross Domestic Product (GDP)

5

5.1 Definition

GDP is the sum total of the value of a country's output over a year. It includes all finished goods and services.

5.2 Real GDP and nominal GDP

Real GDP is GDP adjusted for inflation. Nominal GDP is GDP not adjusted for inflation.

5.3 Limitations of GDP as an indicator of comparative living standards over time

Inflation – to make a proper comparison over time we need to adjust for inflation. It's better to compare real GDP not nominal GDP.

Population growth – to make a proper comparison we need to look at GDP per head not just total GDP.

Quality of goods and services – GDP may grow over time but it doesn't tell us anything about how the quality of goods and services may have changed.

Externalities – GDP may grow over time but it doesn't tell us anything about how external costs may have changed, e.g. pollution, congestion.

5.4 Limitations of GDP as an indicator of comparative living standards between countries

Inflation – different countries have different rates of inflation, therefore we need to compare real GDP not nominal GDP.

Population – some countries have a much larger population than others therefore we need to compare GDP per head not total GDP.

Exchange rate – the figures used to compare GDP are usually in US dollars. Therefore a country's exchange rate against the dollar will influence where it comes in a league table of comparative GDPs.

Problems in collection of data – the compilation of GDP and data collection techniques vary from one country to another. This makes direct comparisons difficult.

Income inequalities – increases in GDP may mean only a small proportion of people have benefited compared to others. Some sense of income distribution needs to be taken into account if the figures are to be meaningful.

Types of commodities being consumed – each country has different needs therefore direct comparisons are difficult, e.g. consumption of energy, fuel and building materials will be higher in a cooler climate than in a warmer climate.

Non-monetarised economy – this is where people exchange goods and services by barter rather than using money, e.g. person X fixes person Y's car if person Y mows person X's lawn. This type of economic activity is higher in developing countries than developed ones but isn't recorded in the figures.

Hidden economy – this varies between countries but in the UK it's estimated to be anywhere between 3-10% of the economy. In Greece it's thought to be about 30%, Spain 25% and Italy 20%.

Purchasing power parity - money can go much further in one country than another. Therefore, we need to take this into account to get a proper comparison. See 5.5 below.

5.5 GDP and purchasing power parity (PPP)

Calculations of GDP at PPP are an attempt to take into account the very different costs of living in different countries, e.g. rent, food, electricity. A worker may get paid substantially more in one country than another, but his costs of living will also be higher.

Taking the IMF figures as a comparison, in 2014 the UK had a GDP per head of $45,563 (ranked 19) and India of $1,627 (ranked 143); but if we look at GDP per head at PPP in the UK it was $39,511 (ranked 27) and India $5,855 (ranked 125), a big difference.

5.6 Measurement of living standards

The standard of living means the level of wealth, material goods and necessities available to the population. The standard measure is GDP per head. An alternative measure is the Human Development Index (see Theme 4), which takes into account life expectancies and education.

5.7 Problems of inaccurate GDP forecasts

Forecast below actual - this means government tax receipts will be below expectations and also more will have to be paid out in benefits than forecast, e.g. JSA, housing benefit. The net effect is that the budget deficit (see 13.1) will grow and this could mean tax increases or spending cuts in the future.

Forecast above actual - this could lead to inflation and the need for the MPC to raise interest rates in the future. Alternatively supply-side policy may need to be expanded to keep up with growth.

Economic growth

6

6.1 Definition

Economic growth means an increase in the productive capacity of the economy. It's measured by increases in real GDP.

6.2 Other measures of economic growth

Gross national product (GNP) - this is GDP plus net property income from abroad. Net property income from abroad means total interest payments, profits and dividends from overseas investment minus interest, profits and dividends earned by foreign investment in the UK.
Gross national income (GNI) - this is GDP plus net property income from abroad, plus net receipts from abroad of wages and salaries.

6.3 Causes of growth

This revolves around the factors of production:

Natural resources – the availability of natural resources such as oil, gas and minerals contributes to growth.
Labour – the numbers of workers available and their skills contributes to growth as do factors such as:

- Education and training – improves human capital
- Increases in the participation rate of women
- Immigration
- Changes in birth rates

Investment – this increases productivity and lowers the average cost of products. It can come from domestic investment or from abroad. This is known as foreign direct investment (FDI).
Technological change – this leads to the availability of bigger and better machines and increased efficiency.
Innovation – this means the invention of new products or ways of doing things. It creates new markets and increases efficiency.

Exports – this creates new markets for a country's products. When this is the predominant component of demand it's called 'export-led growth'.

6.4 Causes of differences in growth rates between countries

Natural resources – different countries have different amounts of natural resources. If you are lucky enough to have large amounts of natural resources your growth rate is likely to be higher, e.g. USA – oil, timber, gas.

Manpower – in order to be able to exploit your natural resources you need the manpower. Countries with large populations are likely to do better than ones with small populations.

Education and training – countries with well-educated populations can keep on increasing their growth because it keeps their economies competitive.

Investment – countries that invest well are likely to have higher growth rates than ones that don't. Investment raises productivity and keeps the economy competitive.

Innovation – countries that can invent new products will experience higher growth rates than ones who don't. Firms can take out patents that give them monopoly rights for a certain amount of years, e.g. 25.

Entrepreneurship – countries with large amounts of entrepreneurs will have higher growth rates than ones that don't. This is why governments often encourage people to start up their own businesses by giving them tax breaks and/or offering advice on how to do it.

6.5 The benefits of growth

Higher living standards – growth creates more jobs. This raises incomes and people's living standards.

Redistribution of wealth – rising incomes means rising tax revenues. This means the government has more to spend on merit goods and benefits.

Lower unemployment – growth creates jobs and reduces unemployment. It also means less has to be spent on benefits, e.g. unemployment benefit.

Improves balance of payments – provided growth is export led it will improve the balance of payments.

Economic growth

Care for the environment – as people get richer they may become more concerned about the environment. This could lead to a better use of resources and reduced external costs.

6.6 Costs of economic growth

External costs – growth can create large amounts of externalities, e.g. pollution, congestion, global warming. These will decrease the quality of life.
Income inequalities – with economic growth there are winners and losers. Gaps between rich and poor may grow.
Inflation – if AD outstrips AS this could lead to higher inflation.
Structural unemployment – rapid growth can leave some people in the economy behind. They can't re-train quickly enough to find jobs in the "new economy".
Balance of payments problems – growth may suck in more imports. This could lead to balance of payments problems.
Social effects – growth is often associated with increased social costs, e.g. crime, vandalism, drug abuse, family breakdown.

6.7 Constraints on growth

Lack of investment – this effects productivity and competitiveness. It also effects innovation and the ability to develop new products and new markets.
Infrastructure – road, rail and air links effect the ability to move goods around the country quickly and also export. It also effects how attractive the country is for foreign investment (FDI). Another important infrastructure requirement is internet access.
Education and training – workers need the right skills to get a job. The UK education system has often been criticised by employers for not being vocational enough. Likewise training programmes at work need to be good enough to keep workers skills up-to-date.
Government policies – these may not encourage competition, innovation and entrepreneurship, e.g. tax policies, deregulation, privatisation.
Access to capital - firms need to be able to find it easy to get funds from banks to grow and expand

6.8 The trade cycle

Economic growth

The trade cycle is the fluctuations in economic activity which happen in an economy over a period of time. The four phases are boom, recession, slump and recovery:

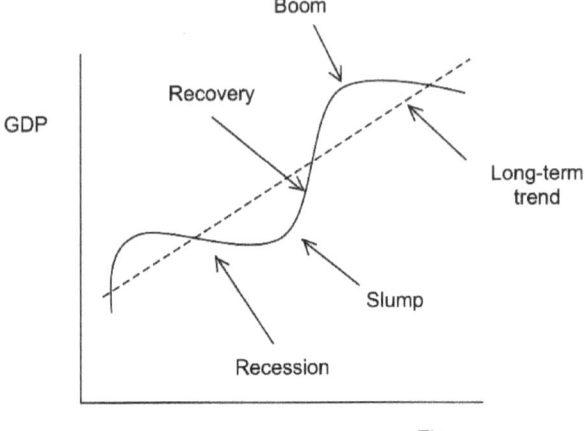

(i) Characteristics of a boom

During a boom the economy is growing in real terms and it's characterised by growths in employment, output and real incomes. Other positive effects include rising investment, tax revenues and business confidence. The negative effects are possible over-heating of the economy causing inflation, and a rise in imports.

(ii) Characteristics of a recession

During a recession the opposite is happening and the economy is contracting in real terms. It will be characterised by rising unemployment, falls in output and falls in real income. Other negative effects include a rising budget deficit because more has to be spent on unemployment benefit, and falling business confidence. A recession can have some positive effects though. These include falling inflation and a falling trade deficit because it means consumers will be spending less on imports. The definition of a recession is below:

Recession - a recession is two successive quarters (or longer) of negative growth. As growth is most often measured by GDP it will mean falling GDP for two or more successive quarters.

6.9 National happiness

Traditionally, economists have tended to measure the success of economies only by looking at monetary values like GDP and incomes. Recently, the Office for National Statistics (ONS) has developed a new range of indicators trying to measure other factors. It has entitled this the National Well-being report. It includes details on:

- Health
- Our relationships
- Personal well-being
- The environment
- Crime/safety
- Education and skills

The idea is to build a broader picture of how happy people feel.

The relationship between real incomes and happiness is a complex one. Undoubtedly higher incomes can improve national well-being, as there are more resources to improve areas such as health and education, but there are negative effects as well such as the impact on the environment and family life.

National Income

7

7.1 Definition

National income is the total value of a country's output of goods and services produced in a year. The usual way to measure it is GDP.

7.2 Ways of calculating national income

Income method – this sums all forms of income earned by factors of production, e.g. wages, profits, rent, interest and dividends. It's the most common way to measure national income.
Expenditure method – this sums consumption, investment, government expenditure and exports less imports [Y = C + I + G + (X-M]
Output method – this sums the value of total output

All three methods in theory should give the same total. In practice there are discrepancies because of problems in collecting the data.

7.3 Circular flow of national income

The circular flow of national income shows how money flows between households and businesses and therefore the inter-connectedness of the economy. See below:

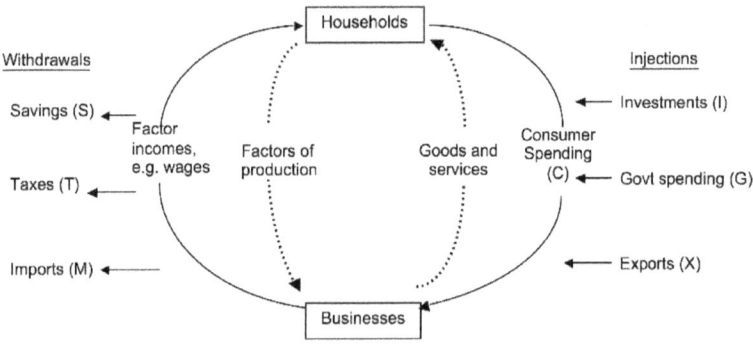

(i) Definitions

Injections – these are money flows which add to the circular flow of income, e.g. business investment, government expenditure.
Withdrawals – these are money flows which take money out of the circular flow of income. They are also known as leakages, e.g. taxes, imports, savings.

(ii) Explanation

We can see how the circular flow of national income works by looking at the diagram above. Households spend their incomes on goods and services provided by businesses. Businesses return this money to households in the form of wages. Along the way there are injections of money into the circular flow in the form of business investment, government spending and exports, and there are also withdrawals in the form of savings, taxation and imports. Money circulates from households to firms and back again, and the more households spend, the more firms produce, and the higher the levels of income. Whatever way you look at it income and output should always be the same and they are measured by GDP.

(iii) The multiplier effect

This refers to the amount by which an injection into the circular flow of income will eventually raise national income. It's given by the multiplier (k). The formula is 1/(1-MPC) where MPC stands for the marginal propensity to consume. Marginal propensity to consume is the proportion of extra income that is spent on consumption. For example let's say the MPC was 0.8 then this would mean the multiplier was 5 [1/(1-0.8)]. So, if the government were to inject £100m into the economy by increasing spending on the NHS this would eventually add £500m to national income. In the UK the size of the multiplier is approximately 1.4.

(iv) Why does an injection into the circular flow of income have a multiplied effect?

The reason why this happens is that the initial injection circulates many times round the economy. Each time some is spent and some is saved or leaks out of the economy in the form of taxes or spending on imports. Using the example above the first time the £100m travels around the economy £80m (£100m x 0.8) will be spent and £20m will be saved (for economists any money that is not spent is 'saved'). The second time £64m (£80m x 0.8) will be spent and £16m will be saved. The third time £51.2m (£64m x 0.8) will be spent and £12.8m will be saved and so on. If we add up all these spending flows and the spending flows of the remaining money we will get £500m. In the UK the size of the multiplier is approximately 1.4, but in developing countries it's often higher which partly explains their higher growth rates.

7.4 Multiplier ratios

In the following abbreviations and formulas 'marginal' means the proportion of extra income, e.g. MPC means the proportion of extra income that is spent on consumption.

(i) Abbreviations

- Marginal propensity to consume (MPC)
- Marginal propensity to save (MPS)
- Marginal propensity to tax (MPT)
- Marginal propensity to import (MPM)
- Marginal propensity to withdraw (MPW)

(ii) Formulas

MPC + MPS = 1
Multiplier (k) = 1/(1-MPC) or 1/MPW
MPW = MPS + MPT + MPM

(iii) Factors effecting size of multiplier

- Propensity to consume
- Propensity to tax
- Propensity to save
- Propensity to import
- Consumer confidence
- Firms ability to expand production to meet extra demand
- Crowding out, e.g. increased government spending may mean increased government borrowing which means there's less funds available for the private sector to invest with.

Aggregate demand (AD)

8

AD is the total amount of spending in the economy. It's the sum of all the individual demand curves.

8.2 Diagram

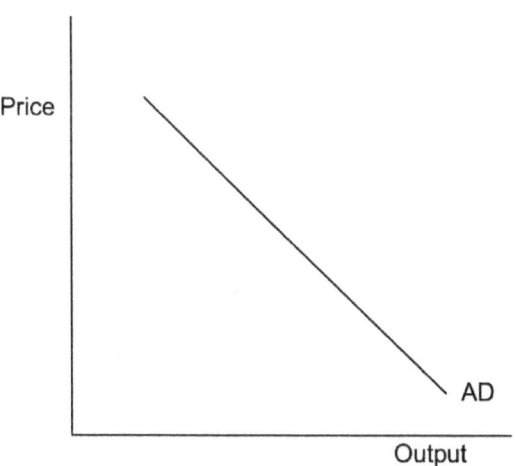

8.3 Reasons why the AD curve slopes downwards

The interest rate argument – as prices increase the interest rate is likely to rise because the government will be trying to slow down inflation. This will decrease investment and consumption and therefore decrease AD. It will also encourage saving and therefore decrease consumption in this way as well.
The international competitiveness argument – lower prices mean increased international competitiveness, so exports increase and imports decrease. As both are components of AD it means AD increases.

8.4 Components

AD can be represented by the following equation:

$$AD = C+I+G+(X-M)$$

From this we can see the components are:

Consumption (C) – this means consumer consumption. It's the largest component and represents about 65% of AD.
Investment (I) - this means business investment and spending on infrastructure. It represents about 15% of AD.
Government spending (G) – this means government spending, e.g. spending on education and health. It represents about 20% of AD.
Exports minus imports (X-M) – this is the balance of payments and represents about -5% of AD because at the moment the UK's imports are bigger than its exports (2014).

8.5 Factors affecting components

(i) Consumption

Income – as incomes rise you would expect consumption to increase.
Interest rate – as the interest rate decreases it increases consumption because loans and credit cards get cheaper to finance. It also means mortgage payments get cheaper therefore households have more disposable income. As the interest rate increases it will have the opposite effect.
Level of saving – if saving increases consumption will fall and vice versa. The level of saving in the economy is called the savings ratio. This is a separate topic in itself and is examined in 8.6 below.
Taxation – if income tax decreases you would expect consumption to rise as it would increase people's disposable incomes and vice–versa.
House prices – house prices effect consumption because of the 'wealth effect'. If house prices are rising then people feel wealthier and increase their consumption. If they are falling consumption decreases.
Consumer confidence - if consumer confidence is high spending will increase. Typically when there's a boom and unemployment is low consumption increases.

(ii) Business investment

There are two reasons why businesses invest. One is to replace worn out fixed assets, such as buildings and plant and machinery.

This is called capital consumption or replacement investment. The other is to buy new capital stock to increase output. This is called net investment.

Two definitions you need to be aware of are:

Gross investment - this means replacement investment plus net investment.
Net investment - this means new investment and is often expressed in the formula, gross investment less depreciation.

The factors affecting business investment are:

Rate of economic growth - if growth is high firms will need to invest more to increase productive capacity to keep up with demand.
Business expectation/confidence - if firms are expecting demand to increase then they will go out and invest more to keep pace with demand. The Keynesian term for business expectations and confidence is 'animal spirits'.
Interest rates – if interest rates fall investment increases because loans are cheaper and vice-versa.
Access to credit - if banks make it easier for firms to borrow money then investment will increase.
Demand for exports - if exports are growing investment will increase as firms seek to increase productive capacity
Business profitability – if profits are rising businesses feel more optimistic about the future and are likely to spend more.
Corporation tax – if corporation tax is cut it means businesses have more money left over for investment. Therefore investment ought to increase and vice-versa.

(iii) Government spending

Changes in government policy – if the government wants to improve public services like education and health then this would increase government spending.
Trade cycle – during a recession government spending tends to increase because more money has to be spent on transfer payments, e.g. unemployment benefit. During a recovery/boom it tends to decrease because employment levels are high and less has to be spent on benefits.

(iv) Exports and imports

Real incomes - as incomes rise imports tend to increase. We often see this during growth periods in the economy. This is because the UK has a high marginal propensity to import (MPM). Most manufactured goods in the UK are imported, so as peoples' incomes increase and they seek to increase their standard of living, this sucks in more imports.

Exchange rate – a fall in the exchange rate makes exports cheaper and imports more expensive. A rise in the exchange rates does the opposite. Therefore, when the exchange rate falls you could expect exports to rise, but if the exchange rate rises you would expect exports to fall.

Interest rates – interest rates and the exchange tend to move in the same direction. If interest rates rise this would increase demand for sterling and push the exchange rate up. There is an increase of what are known as "hot money" flows into the country as investors try to take advantage of higher interest rates in the UK to increase the return on their deposits. This would make exports more expensive and imports cheaper. If the interest rate fell the opposite would happen.

Elasticities of demand for exports and imports - if demand for exports is inelastic then a rise in the price wouldn't affect demand that much. The same would be true of imports. Likewise when demand for exports or imports is elastic then demand will be much more sensitive to price changes.

State of world economy - if the world economy is going through a downturn then exports will fall because demand will be low. Likewise at home, imports will fall as consumers seek to rein in spending because they fear losing their jobs.

Degree of protectionism - if tariff barriers and quota restrictions are high in other countries this will hit exports.

Non-price factors - these are factors such as quality, brand names and product features. If these are better in other countries it will suck in imports.

8.6 Savings ratio

(i) Definition

The savings ratio is the percentage of disposable income which is saved.

(ii) Factors effecting savings ratio

Interest rates - if interest rates rise you would expect people to save more and spend less.

Levels of income - as incomes rise people can afford to save more.

Wealth - as personal wealth increases so does consumer confidence and so people feel as if they can run down their savings, e.g. during a boom in the housing market - wealth effect.

State of the economy - during a boom people feel confident about their job security and so feel as if they can spend more and save less. During a recession the opposite will happen, people will feel as if they might lose their job and so start saving just in case they need to rely on savings.

Income inequalities - people on low incomes tend to save less than people on high incomes because they have to spend nearly everything they earn on necessities. Therefore, if gaps between rich and poor widen you would expect the savings ratio to fall.

Availability of credit - if credit is easy to obtain it encourages further spending. It counts as dis-saving.

(iii) Importance of savings ratio

Consumption - if savings rise consumption will fall and so it effects AD and growth.

Investment - the higher the savings ratio the more money banks can lend to firms for investment, so again it effects growth.

Aggregate Supply (AS)

9

9.1 Definition

The total amount of goods and services produced in the economy.

9.2 Short-run aggregate supply (SRAS)

(i) Shape of curve

SRAS assumes that at least one factor input is held constant. This is normally the capital stock, i.e. factories, plant and machinery. In the short-run SRAS is elastic as firms can run down stocks to satisfy demand and take on extra workers to increase output. It slopes upwards to the right indicating firms are willing to supply more as the price increases. See below:

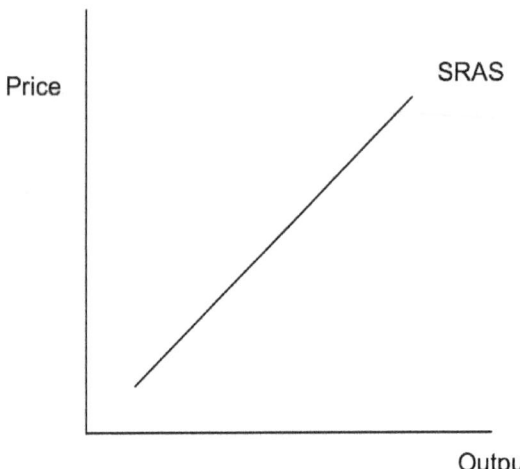

(ii) Factors influencing SRAS

- Costs of production - e.g. labour, raw materials, energy
- Changes in exchange rates - this can effect the cost of imported components and raw materials
- Changes in tax rates - e.g. corporation tax, income tax. These effect the incentive to work and invest.

9.3 Long-run aggregate supply (LRAS)

The LRAS curve assumes all factors of production can vary. There are two views on its shape.

(i) Classical view

According to the classical view, the LRAS curve is vertical because the assumption is the economy has reached its full potential output level. Any increase in demand will only increase the price level and can't lead to any increases in AS, as all resources in the economy have been fully utilised.

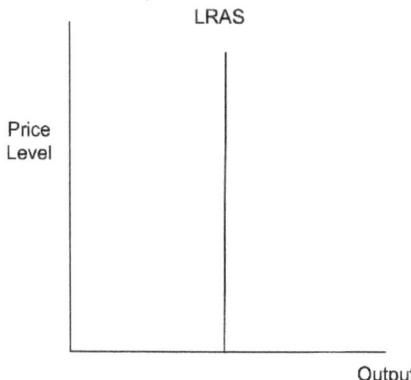

(ii) Keynesian view

The Keynesian view is that the classical economists have oversimplified the LRAS curve. Keynes felt that there could be increases in AD without significant increases or perhaps any increases in the price level, so he felt it was L-shaped.

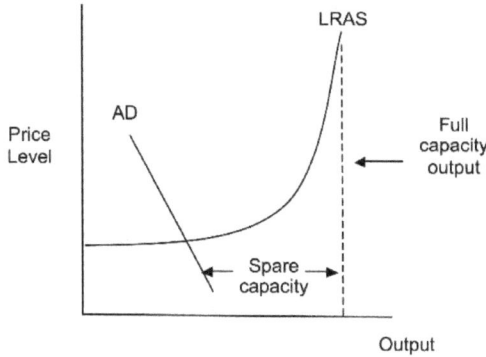

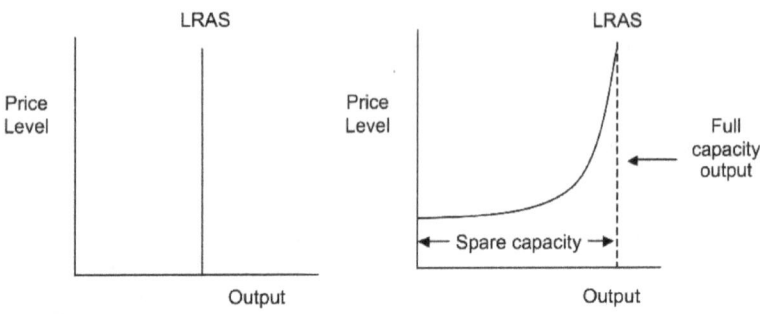

9.4 The output gap

(i) Definition and diagrams

The output gap is the difference between potential output and actual output. We can show it on the diagram below where Q_1 is the actual level of output and Q_2 the potential level of output. Another way to show it is by using PPF curves where point A (actual output) is a point within the PPF curve, and B (potential output) is a point on the curve.

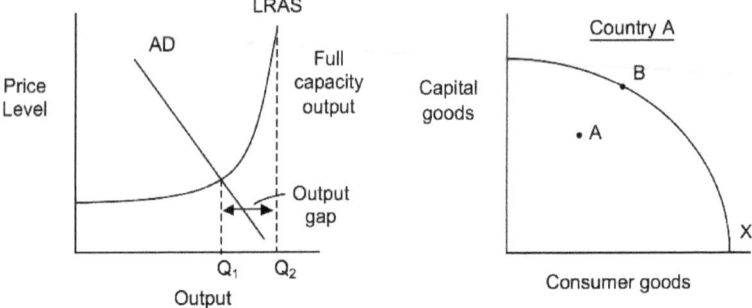

An output gap means there is scope for growth in the economy and there are unused factors of production, e.g. labour, raw materials, capital. It's also known as spare capacity. Yet another way to show it, is the diagram below:

Aggregate supply

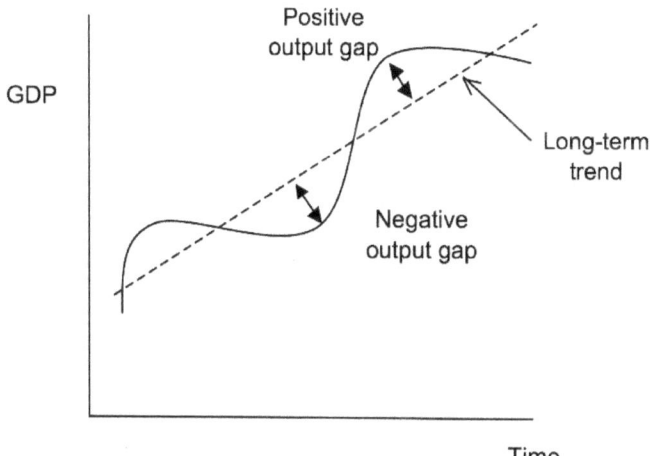

(ii) Positive and negative output gaps

Negative output gap - this is when actual output is below potential output. There will be spare capacity in the economy and it will be characterised by low growth and unemployment. It's also known as the deflationary gap. Another feature is the downward pressure on inflation.
Positive output gap - this is when actual output is above potential output. It will create inflationary pressure in the economy. Another feature is likely to be a widening trade deficit, as consumer spending increases and sucks in more imports.

(iii) Difficulties in measuring the output gap

Different economists come up with different figures for the output gap at any point in time. The government has its own estimates, but these differences cause major discussions about whether the government is pursuing the right economic policies.

9.5 Distinction between a shift in the AD/AS curves and a movement along them

This is the same as for microeconomics. If only price is changing you are moving along the curve, but if there are changes in the conditions of AD or AS then the whole curve moves either to the left or right.

Equilibrium level of real output

10

10.1 Definition

The equilibrium level of real output occurs when AD equals AS. See below:

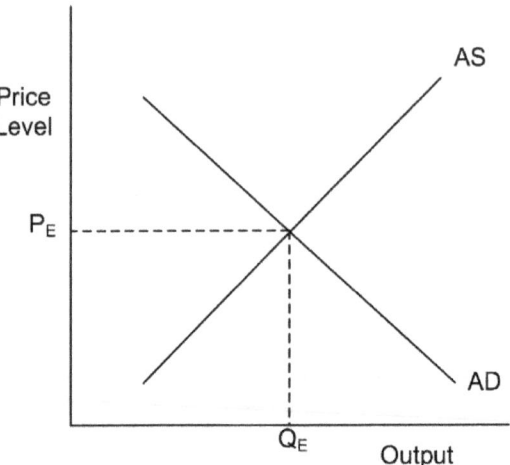

10.2 AD/AS questions

There are always AD/AS questions in the exam. They can be either short or long. The difference is that with the short ones there's usually little or no evaluation and you use the normal AD/AS curves whereas with the long questions there's a lot of evaluation and you are supposed to use the L-shaped LRAS curve. See below for examples:

(i) What would be the effect on the price level and level of real output if there was an increase in the level of investment?

Equilibrium output

Short answer

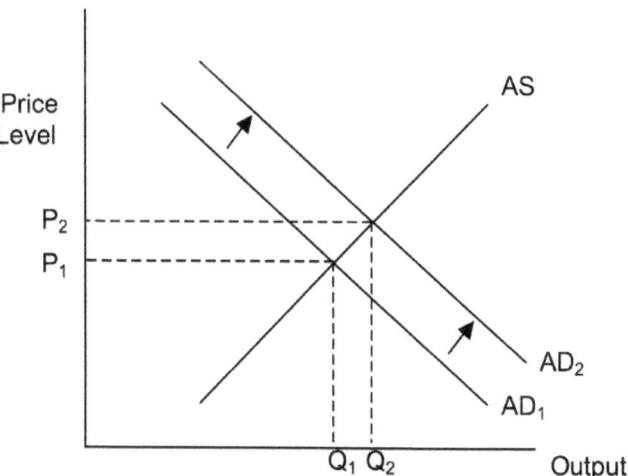

If business investment increases it will shift the AD curve to the right because investment is a component of AD. This will increase the price level and also the level of real output (AD_1–AD_2). It will also have an effect on AS in the long run because investment will raise productivity. This will shift the AS curve to the right lowering the price level and raising output.

Long Answer

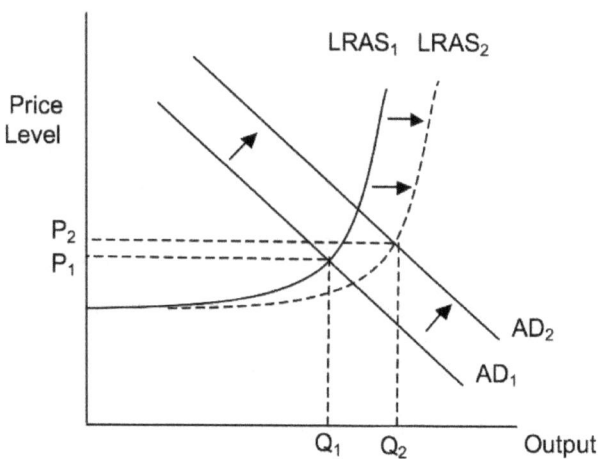

For the long answer you would say exactly the same but you would use the LRAS curves and have two or three evaluation points. For example:

Evaluation

Effect on price level and level of real output depends on:

- How much investment takes place.
- Whether there's spare capacity or not, i.e. how elastic/inelastic LRAS is.
- Depends on whether there are falls in the other components of AD, e.g. consumption, exports or an increase in imports. These might cancel out the effect of an increase in investment.

(ii) What would be the effect on the price level and the real level of output if interest rates fell?

Short answer

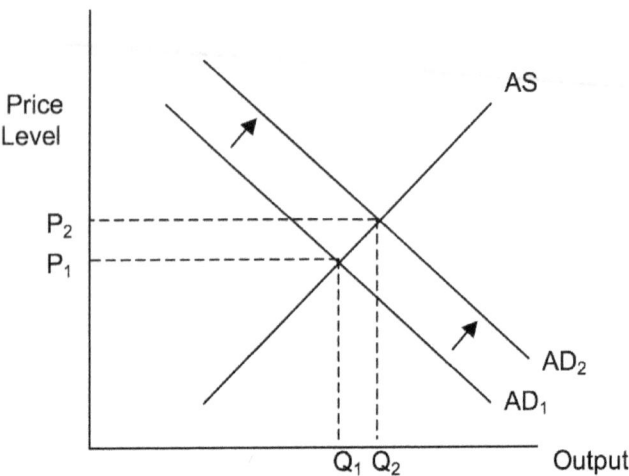

A decrease in the interest rate will increase consumption because it will make mortgages cheaper and increase disposable incomes. It will also increase consumption because borrowing will get cheaper and people might spend more on their credit cards. The net result is that AD will shift to the right ($AD_1 - AD_2$) and increase the price level (P_1-P_2) and the level of real output (Q_1-Q_2).

See above

Long Answer

For the long answer say the same but examine the effects on the supply-side and evaluate as well:

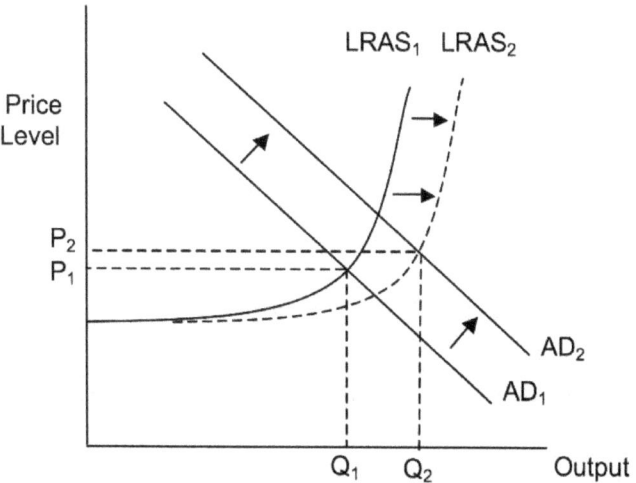

Supply-side effects

There will also be effects on the supply side although this might take longer to feed through. A decrease in interest rates will make borrowing for firms cheaper and therefore it will encourage investment. This will shift the AS curve to the right shifting the price level down and increasing the level of real output.

Evaluation

- Depends on how much interest rates fall by and for how long.
- Depends on how much spare capacity there is, i.e. how elastic/inelastic LRAS is.

(iii) What would be the effect on the price level and a level of real output if there was an increase in the oil price?

Short answer

Equilibrium output

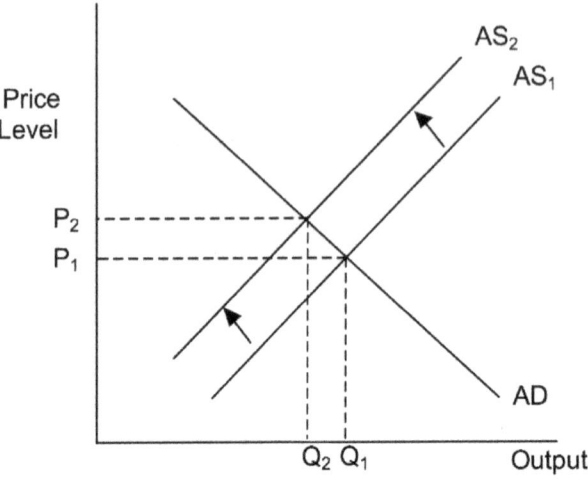

An increase in the price of oil will increase production costs. This will shift AS to the left (AS_1-AS_2) and increase the price level (P_1-P_2) and decrease level of real output (Q_1-Q_2). On the demand side AD will shift to the left because it may mean higher prices in the shops and therefore reduced consumption.

Long answer

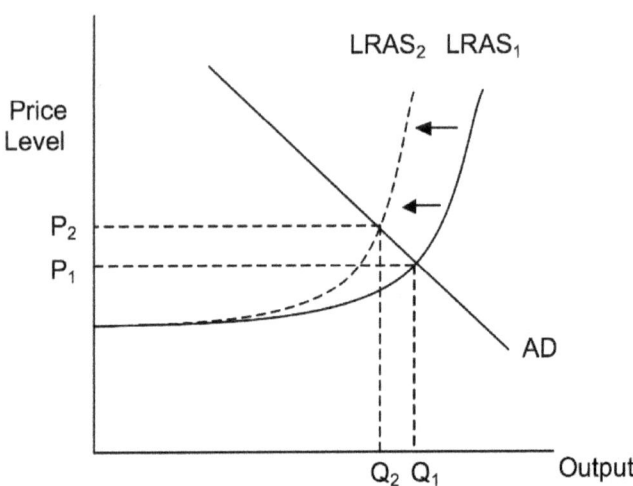

For the long answer say the same as before but evaluate as well:

Evaluation

- Depends on how much the oil price goes up by and for how long.
- Depends on the ability of firms to absorb the extra costs by making savings elsewhere, e.g. raw materials, labour, increases in productivity through investment.
- Depends on degree of competition in product markets.
- Depends on strength of consumer demand – they may ignore price increases and keep on spending, e.g. if interest rates are low.
- The fall in AD might cancel out the inflationary effects of the increase in costs – but growth will slow.

(iv) What would be the effect of a stock market fall on the price level and level of real output?

Short answer

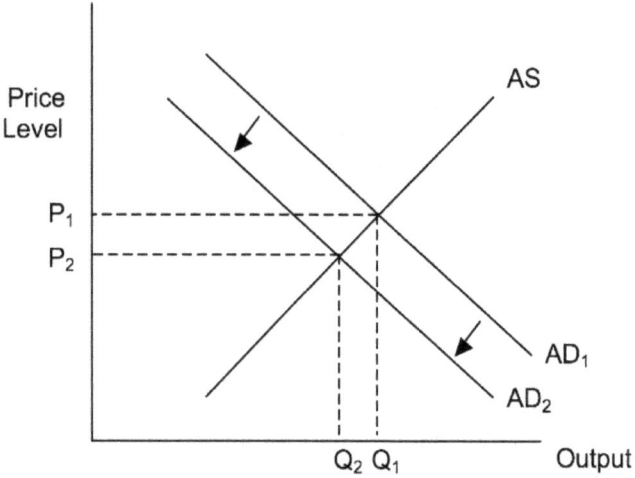

If there was a big stock market fall AD would shift to the left (AD_1-AD_2). This is because consumers may fear losing their jobs and therefore they would reduce consumption in order to 'save for a rainy day'. They might also have money invested on the stock market and therefore it would have a negative effect on the 'wealth effect' and spending.

Long answer

For the long answer say the same thing as the above but discuss the effect on business investment and evaluate as well:

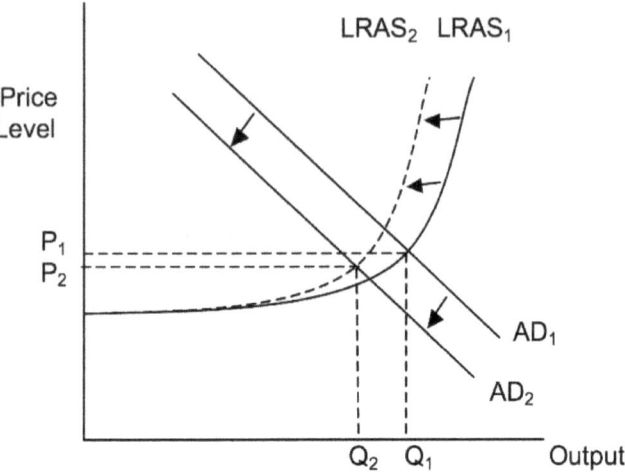

Effect on business investment

Businesses would also feel more nervous about investing because they think consumers will spend less. This will have an effect on both AD and AS. It will shift both of these to the left as it reduces AD on one hand, and reduces productivity on the other.

Evaluation

- Depends on how much the stock market falls by and how long it lasts.
- Depends on consumer confidence – if house prices are rising and there's low unemployment then consumers may keep on spending because they think the 'crisis' will quickly pass.
- Other things may not be equal, e.g. if government spending is rising at the same time or interest rates are low encouraging consumption these would cancel out any effect on AD of a stock market fall. Remember AD = C + I + G + (X-M).

Government's economic objectives

11

There are seven of these:

- Low and stable Inflation
- Low unemployment
- Economic growth (GDP)
- Balance of payments equilibrium on current account
- Redistribution of income
- Balanced government budget
- Protection of the environment

Let's look at these one by one. GDP and economic growth have already been covered in sections 5 and 6, and the government budget will be covered in section 13. Externalities will not be covered specifically, but rather topic-by-topic as it occurs.

11.1 Inflation

(i) Definition

Inflation is a sustained increase in the general price level.

(ii) Causes

There are three causes of inflation:

Demand-pull inflation – this is where excess demand pushes up prices.

Cost-push inflation – this is where rising costs force firms to increase prices to protect profit margins.

Growth of the money supply - this is where excessive growth of the money supply leads to banks lending more to borrowers, which in turn leads to more spending and an increase in inflation.

(iii) Problems of inflation

Unemployment – an increase in costs reduces profitability. Firms might react to this by cutting jobs and therefore creating unemployment.

Loss of international competitiveness – if UK inflation is higher than other countries this could make our exports less competitive. This would then have a knock-on effect on balance of payments.
Reduced spending and investment – inflation creates a climate of uncertainty. Consumers are reluctant to spend and businesses are reluctant to invest until the uncertainty passes.
Lower growth – increased unemployment, reduced spending and investment, and lower exports all shift AD to the left. This reduces growth.
Increase in "shoe leather costs" and "menu costs" – businesses spend more time looking around for the best deal (shoe leather costs) and also spend more time updating price lists and catalogues (menu costs).
Redistribution of wealth from savers to borrowers – inflation tends to favour borrowers not savers. This is because it reduces the value of loans (i.e. favours borrowers) but reduces the value of savings at the same time (i.e. penalises savers).

(iv) Benefits of mild inflation

Rising revenues and profits – higher prices mean increased revenue and profits for business. It also encourages them to invest more.
Increased spending – workers will receive good pay increases. This will encourage them to spend more.
Decreases value of loans – businesses will see the value of their loans decrease and consumers will see the value of their mortgages decrease. This increases business investment and consumer spending.
Increases house prices – an increase in house prices makes people feel wealthier (the "wealth effect"). Therefore they are more likely to go out and spend.

(v) Problems of falling prices

Disinflation means prices are still rising but at a slower rate, deflation means that prices are falling, i.e. the rate of inflation is negative. Recently, there has been much talk about the negative effects these could have on the UK economy, as for some time inflation has been very low and even negative. Specifically, economists have worried about the following:

Delayed consumer spending - if consumers think the price will be cheaper next month they may delay spending. This could have a knock-on effect on growth and jobs.
Delayed investment - if businesses notice an effect on demand they will delay investment. This could effect growth, jobs and competitiveness.

11.2 Unemployment

(i) Types of unemployment

Frictional – this occurs when people are moving between jobs. It's the time delay between losing one job and finding another.
Search – this is similar to frictional unemployment but occurs because people are searching for the right job. Therefore, they may turn down one job and wait for a better offer.
Seasonal – occurs because some jobs are highly seasonal, e.g. catering, tourism, agriculture.
Structural – occurs because of structural changes in the economy, e.g. de-industrialisation in the UK in the 1970's and 1980's.
Cyclical – this occurs because of changes in the trade cycle, i.e. during recessions.

Causes

There are two causes of unemployment:

Wage-rate unemployment – this is where the wage rate is above the equilibrium rate (W_E). This causes an excess of supply of labour (Q_1-Q_2). See below:

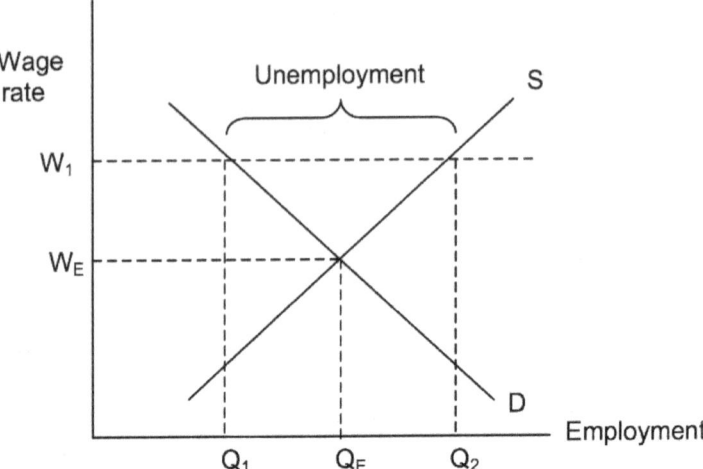

Cyclical unemployment (demand deficient unemployment) – this type of unemployment occurs when there's a recession in the economy. The lack of demand creates unemployment.

<u>(ii) Effects</u>

Increases government spending – unemployment means the government has to spend more on benefits, e.g. JSA, housing benefit.

Increased government borrowing – unemployment means the government is receiving less in income tax and paying out more in benefits. It therefore may have to borrow more to pay for it.

Lower growth – unemployment represents a waste of labour resources. GDP will be lower and growth will be slower than if all the labour resources were fully utilised. There will also be lower consumption shifting AD to the left.

Social costs – unemployment is usually associated with higher crime rates, divorce and health problems.

<u>(iii) Impact of immigration on employment/unemployment</u>

Emigration is when people leave the country. Immigration is when people come into the country. In the past 5 years there has been net migration of about 1m people into the UK. You should be aware of the impact of this on the labour market.

Advantages

- Migrants help to keep the labour market competitive – therefore UK firms can keep costs low and grow. This creates more jobs in the future.
- Migrants help to fill skills gaps in the economy and help it be more productive, e.g. nurses, construction workers, doctors, IT workers
- May make the UK more attractive for foreign investment as it holds wages down on one hand and fills skills gaps on the other. This creates more jobs.
- Increased consumption by migrants might create more jobs

Disadvantages

- Migrants provide competition for UK workers so they might displace UK workers from their jobs creating unemployment.
- Migrants often have lower expectations of wages – therefore they might help to keep wages low and undermine the ability of unions to get higher wages.
- Migrants might end up working in the hidden economy – therefore the UK develops a dual labour market, which keeps wages low.
- Migrants and their families put added pressure on public services e.g. education, health, housing. Therefore, this requires more government borrowing or higher taxes.

11.3 Balance of payments

In general, the government tries to run a small trade surplus. Having a large trade deficit is seen as something to avoid.

(i) Causes of a trade deficit

Lack of competitiveness - e.g. quality, cost, design, lack of investment, lack of training.
Inflation – UK inflation may be higher than in other countries therefore costs and prices are higher.
Exchange rate – may be too high therefore exports are too expensive.

Economic growth - rising incomes and employment may mean more imports are sucked into the country. The UK has a high MPM.
Government policies, e.g.

- Monetary policy - interest rates may be set high to control inflation but this will raise the exchange rate and therefore make exports more expensive.
- Supply-side policy - not enough being done to improve training.
- Fiscal policy - taxes too high decreasing incentives to work and investment.

(ii) Problems of having a large deficit

Higher unemployment – a trade deficit means that imports are higher than exports and therefore jobs are probably being lost in manufacturing.
Higher inflation – a trade deficit could lead to a falling exchange rate. This could mean import costs would go up and could result in "imported inflation".
Fall in GDP - a balance of payments deficit is a withdrawal from the circular flow of income. Therefore, it causes a fall in growth.
Loss of long-term competitiveness – this could lead to lower living standards in the future, as there may be fewer jobs and therefore lower incomes.
Increase in government borrowing – there may be an increase in government borrowing to support the exchange rate in a fixed exchange rate system. This could effect government spending on public services.

(iii) Is having a trade deficit a cause for concern?

If you are asked this question in the exam first of all comment on the problems of having a large deficit then raise these evaluative points:

- It depends on how big the deficit is and how long it persists - e.g. the balance of payments is cyclical therefore it may not be a cause for concern.
- It depends on whether there's a surplus on trade in services to balance it out.

- It depends on what the imports are. If they are mainly of capital goods and therefore for investment this may improve the long-term competitiveness of the economy and reverse the deficit in the future.

<u>11.4 Redistribution of income</u>

<u>(i) Causes of income inequality</u>

Differences in occupation – some people do high earning jobs, others low earning jobs e.g. doctors vs. security guard.
Differences in education and qualifications – some people have better qualifications than others therefore they can earn more.
Unemployment – people who are unemployed will only receive state benefits therefore their income will be much below average.
Retirement – people who are retired will be living on their pensions therefore their incomes will be below average.
Physical and financial wealth – people who have inherited wealth will be able to get income from unearned sources as well as a job, e.g. interest, dividends, rent. This will cause income inequalities.
Government policies – the government can influence inequalities through the tax and benefit system.
Others – this list isn't exhaustive and could include:

- Gender
- Discrimination
- Disability
- Regional cost of living

<u>(ii) Problems of income inequalities</u>

Higher government spending – to make up the difference and even out inequalities e.g. JSA, housing benefit, pensions.
Lower demand – larger gaps between rich and poor may mean demand is lower. The poor have less money to spend and this could affect growth.
Political problems – larger gaps between rich and poor may mean more strikes and political instability.

<u>(iii) Arguments for income inequalities</u>

The main argument for income inequalities is that it creates an incentive for the workforce. Wealth creators need an incentive otherwise no one would start their own businesses and the economy would be worse off. If taxes are too high it will also affect productivity and costs.

(iv) The difference between income and wealth

Income – this is the amount of money a person gets from his or her job (earned income). It also includes income from financial assets, e.g. interest, rent (unearned income).
Wealth – this is the stock of assets owned by a person, e.g. house, savings, pension. In the UK, housing is most people's most important asset and accounts for about 35% of the UK's wealth

Government economic policies

12

There are 3 types:

- Fiscal policy
- Monetary policy
- Supply-side policy

Let's look at these one by one.

12.1 Fiscal policy

(i) Definition

Fiscal policies are economic policies designed to manage the level of AD in the economy by changing government spending, taxation and borrowing.

(ii) Examples

- To reduce unemployment the government might increase government spending to increase AD and create a multiplier effect across the economy.
- To reduce inflation the government might increase income tax to reduce demand
- To redistribute income the government might reduce income tax for lower income groups.

(iii) Evaluation

There are several evaluation issues you can raise in questions:

Time lags – it takes times for taxation and government spending changes to work. Typically it's between 6 and 12 months.
Inflation – if AD is increased when the economy is working at full capacity, it can create inflation.
Crowding out – too much government spending diverts resources away from the private sector and weakens it.
Lack of flexibility – if the government commits itself to large scale spending it's very difficult not to carry out even if the economy improves in the meantime and it's no longer necessary, e.g.

spending on schools and hospitals. Government taxation and spending plans can also only be reviewed once a year on budget day.

Incomplete information and statistics – much government information is incomplete. It's easy to miscalculate the effects of tax cuts and government spending.

'Stop-go' effect – by attempting to fine-tune the economy using fiscal policy the government can create a 'stop-go' effect. First they might try to accelerate the economy, and then try to slow it down. This makes it difficult for business to plan ahead and deters investment.

(iv) Expansionary and contractionary fiscal policy

Expansionary fiscal policy means policies to encourage growth in the economy, e.g. increase government spending. The government has been doing this during the financial crisis to keep the economy afloat. Contractionary fiscal policy means policies to slow down growth in the economy, e.g. the government might rein in public spending during a boom to prevent the economy overheating and slow down inflation.

12.2 Monetary Policy

(i) Definition

Monetary policy is concerned with the adjustment of interest rates and the money supply in order to control the level of spending in the economy. These days it's mostly about adjusting interest rates rather doing anything to the money supply.

(ii) Monetary Policy Committee (MPC)

In 1997 Gordon Brown took the interest rate decision out of the hands of the Treasury and gave it to the Monetary Policy Committee of the Bank of England. This is a committee of 9 leading economists (including the governor and deputy governor of the Bank of England) and they meet once a month to set interest rates. They are given an inflation target, currently 2%, at the beginning of the fiscal year (5 April) and they must keep to it by ±1 %. If they miss the target they have to write a letter of explanation to the Chancellor of the Exchequer. The range of data they look at is examined below in (iv).

(iii) Benefits of the MPC

Interest rate decision won't be motivated by political factors – in the past when the interest rate decision was taken by the Treasury, the government was often influenced by political factors, e.g. just before a general election the government might reduce interest rates to create a mini-boom so people would vote for them. If it's taken out of the hands of the politicians this won't happen. **Better quality decisions –** the MPC committee members are all experts in their field therefore we should get a better quality decision.

(iv) Data the MPC look at

The role of the MPC is to deliver price stability and subject to that to support the government's other economic objectives such as growth and unemployment. To do this it looks at a whole range of data as listed below. If you are asked this question in the exam just think of the government's economic objectives and the components of AD and you won't go far wrong.

- Unemployment
- Consumption
- Business investment
- Government spending
- Wages growth
- House prices
- Imports/exports
- Present rate of inflation
- Consumer confidence
- Manufacturing output
- Trend in GDP
- Trend in stock market

(v) MPC exam questions

Below are some typical exam questions on the MPC. The best way to answer them is to turn them into an AD/AS question and draw a diagram, e.g.

(a) Why might the claimant count measure of unemployment be significant to the Monetary Policy Committee? (6 marks)

Answer: The claimant count measure of unemployment would be significant to the MPC because it effects consumption. If unemployment were falling it would mean consumption was rising and if inflation were close to target it would encourage the MPC to raise interest rates to head off inflation. This is because consumption is a component of AD and therefore AD would be shifting to the right.

(b) How might an increase in house prices affect the MPC's decision on interest rates? (8 marks)

Answer: An increase in house prices would probably encourage the MPC to raise interest rates. This is because it would create a "wealth effect" improving consumer confidence and therefore consumers would spend more. In turn this would increase consumption and shift AD to the right. If inflation were close to target it would therefore encourage the MPC to raise interest rates. A lot would depend though on how much house prices increased by and if the MPC thought it was sustainable. Also it might be cancelled out by other factors such as cuts in government spending.

(vi) Evaluation of monetary policy questions in general

When evaluating questions that involve monetary policy think about the following points:

- How much does the interest rate go up or down by, e.g. 0.25%, 0.5%.
- How long will it last, e.g. 1 month, 3 months,1 year
- Time lag – consumers and businesses take time to react to interest rate changes. The Bank of England puts it at about two years before the full effects are felt.
- Knock-on effects – the interest rate affects the exchange rate. They usually move in the same direction. Therefore adjustment to the interest rate will often affect the balance of payments as well.
- Effect on house prices – adjustments to the interest rate affect mortgage payments. Therefore think about the effect on house prices and the wealth effect.

(vii) Effects of interest rate changes on income inequalities

This is another type of question that can be tricky to answer. To answer it, think about the effect of interest rate changes on:

- Savings – particularly those of pensioners who make up the biggest group of those on low incomes.
- Borrowing – particularly mortgages.
- Growth – particularly jobs.
- Inflation

It's a difficult one to give a set answer to because no matter what the question, interest rates rising or falling, it can be argued both ways. The essential thing is that you use economic logic. Here is one answer you can use and adapt, but as mentioned it would be possible to argue the opposite as long as you use good economic reasoning.

Question

What might be the effect of falling interest rates on income inequalities? (8 marks)

Answer: Falling interest rates would probably reduce income inequalities because it would encourage consumption and create more jobs. Consumers would find it cheaper to borrow money on credit cards and loans and therefore with more spending in the shops it would reduce unemployment. Wages are higher then benefits therefore income inequalities would get smaller. Having said this falling interest rates would also mean savers would suffer, particularly those on low fixed incomes like pensioners, therefore some of this effect would be cancelled out.

(viii) Quantitative easing (QE)

This is a new type of monetary policy the Bank of England began in 2009 in response to the financial crisis of 2008. It entails the Central Bank buying up government bonds (gilts) and corporate bonds from commercial banks and other financial institutions. Because the banks have now got more cash, it should incentivise them to go out and lend more to small/medium sized businesses, and individuals, and thereby stimulate the economy. To date the government has made QE purchases of £375bn.

Evaluation

- **Banks have still been reluctant to lend** – initially banks just used it as a way to rebuild their balance sheets and sit on the money. They were only lending to big companies not the small/medium ones. The government tried to get around this problem by introducing the Funding for Lending Scheme (FLS) in 2012, which attached conditions to the funding, encouraging more lending to smaller businesses, but this hasn't been entirely successful.
- **Could create inflation** – the quantity theory of money suggests that at some point QE will create inflation. Having said that countries that have used it haven't found this – at least not yet.
- **Could depreciate the currency** – it might create 'imported inflation' but it does have the positive side-effect of making exports cheaper.

12.3 Supply- side policies

(i) Definition

Supply side policies are policies that are designed to encourage the free working of product and factor markets and increase aggregate supply.

(ii) Diagram

Government economic policies

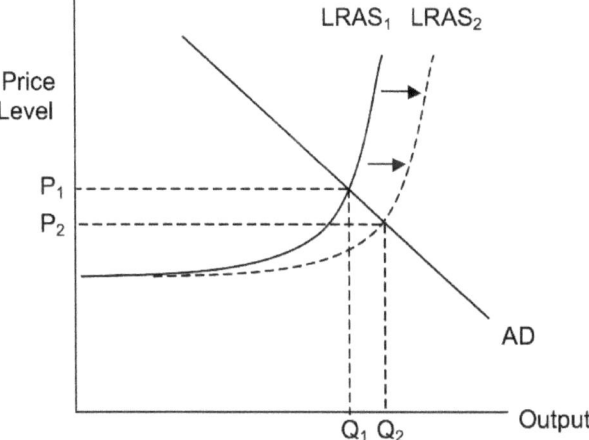

The idea is to increase aggregate supply and therefore reduce prices and increase output at the same time. See above.

(iii) Policies

(a) Tax cuts - e.g. income tax, corporation tax.

Cuts in income tax would increase the incentive to work. Cuts in corporation tax would increase the incentive to invest and for people to start their own business. Both of these would increase supply.

Evaluation

- May reduce tax revenues - therefore there is less money available for spending on merit goods, e.g. education, health. This would decrease AS in the long-run.
- May cause widening gaps between rich and poor.
- Corporation tax cuts may just mean bigger dividends for shareholders, not extra reinvestment in the business.

(b) Cuts in benefit

This means freezing/reducing benefits and/or making it more difficult for people to claim them. It ought to increase the incentive to work and therefore increase supply.

Evaluation

51

- May cause widening gaps between rich and poor.
- Workers need to have jobs to go to if its to work

(c) Increase training

This means having government training programmes to train people to fill skill shortages, e.g. plumbers, electricians, I.T. workers.

Evaluation

- Quality of training programmes may not be good enough.
- May have to raise taxes to pay for training programmes.
- Time lag – takes time to work.
- Workers need to have jobs to go to

(d) Educational reforms

This means improving access to higher education and/or making it more vocational.

Evaluation

- Money may be wasted on creating more university places but graduates may still not be able to get a job because they haven't got the right skills, e.g. Madonna Studies
- Time lag – takes time to work.

(e) Trade union reform

This means reducing union power so they can't interfere in how the labour market works.

Evaluation

- Much of the legislation already exists so it's difficult to think of new legislation the government could bring in to make things better.

(f) Others

- Improving transport and infrastructure

- Improving health and education
- Tax breaks for investment or research and development (R&D)

(iv) General evaluation point

- Supply-side policy doesn't work if the economy is functioning below full capacity or if AD is weak. All we would get in this case is increasing AS but little increase in AD. See below:

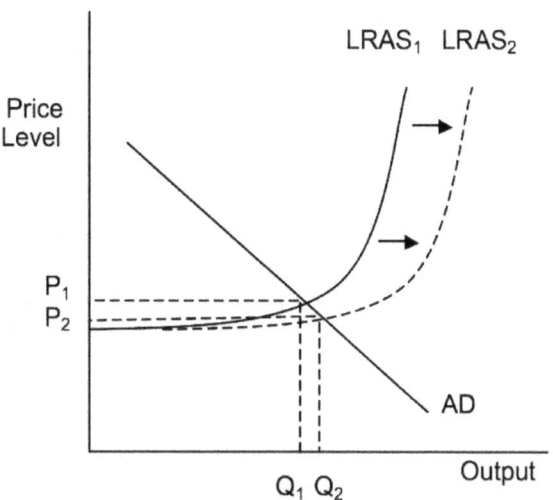

12.4 Demand-side policies used in the Great Depression and Global Financial Crisis 2008

(i) Great Depression

The economic orthodoxy in the 1930's was to have balanced budgets. It was thought that governments could do little to influence jobs and incomes. This explains the initial reluctance for governments in the US and UK to increase government spending to avert a crisis. It wasn't until Roosevelt's New Deal in 1933, that governments took seriously the Keynesian view, that government borrowing and spending, and the multiplier effect could keep the economy afloat. In fact in 1931 the UK government cut public sector wages and raised income tax to balance the budget which only made the situation worse.

In terms of monetary policy, the lessons learnt were to cut interest rates early and by large amounts, and to bail out the banks to prevent bank failures. In the US its estimated between 1930-33 10,000 banks either failed or were suspended.

(ii) Global Financial Crisis

At the start of the financial crisis the Bank of England base rate was 5%. Within weeks of the crisis breaking it was being cut. Eventually by March 2009 it was only 0.5%. The idea was to stimulate spending and investment, and restore confidence. When this didn't work, the bank began using quantitative easing. To date it has injected £375bn into the economy.

In terms of fiscal policy the then Labour government cut VAT from 17.5% to 15% temporarily to stimulate spending, and also brought forward about £3bn of capital spending. At the same time large amounts of money were used to bail out the banks. The final total cost of this was estimated at loans, guarantees and bank purchases of £850bn. Just before they lost power they introduced a top rate of income tax of 50% to increase tax revenues.

The Coalition government responded to the deteriorating budget position by raising VAT to 20% and making spending cuts, although the NHS, education and foreign aid were ring-fenced. The top rate of income tax was cut to 45% in 2013 and corporation tax fell from 28% to 20% over the period the Coalition were in power.

In the US the policy responses have been similar. At the start of the crisis the Federal Reserve funds rate was about 6% but by late 2008 it had been slashed to 0.25%, where it's remained ever since. In terms of QE there have been three rounds to date totalling $4.5trn.

Public spending and taxation

13

Public spending means government spending on public goods and merit goods, e.g.

- Health
- Education
- Housing
- Transport
- Social security

The largest single item of public spending is on social security, e.g. job seekers allowance, child benefit and pensions. It accounts for about 35% of public spending. Health and education are the next biggest items accounting for about 10-12% of public spending each.

13.1 Budget surpluses, budget deficits and national debt

Budget surplus – this means that government tax receipts exceed government spending.
Budget deficit – this means that government spending exceeds government tax receipts. It's also known as the fiscal deficit.
National debt – this is the accumulation of budget deficits over the years. The budget deficit (2014) is currently running at around £110 bn per year and the national debt is around £1.2 trn. This is about 75% of GDP. A normal figure would be about 40% of GDP; the unusually high figure is because of the financial crisis which started in 2008.

13.2 Office for Budget Responsibility (OBR)

The OBR was formed in 2010. Its function is to provide independent economic forecasts ahead of the government's budget and to analyse and report on the sustainability of public finances. The advantage is because it's independent it shouldn't be swayed by political factors.

13.3 Problem of high national debt

- May have to raise taxes later to pay it off - this would slow down economic growth in the future.
- May have to make government spending cuts to pay it off - this would effect the quality of public services and the amount that could be spent on benefits.
- Higher national debt may only be cyclical rather than structural - may be due to recession, rather than an underlying problem. When there is a recovery in the economy it could go down again.
- Loss of AAA credit rating - this could lead to higher interest rates generally, effecting mortgage payments and consumption as well as investment.
- Interest payments – there's an opportunity cost in servicing the debt, e.g. UK debt interest was £35bn in 2015, about the same as the defence budget. In some cases the interest payments are so high a country may have a problem paying off the capital.
- Crowding out - too many resources are being diverted to government sector projects, such as building schools and hospitals thus depriving the private sector of labour, capital and raw materials (resource crowding out). This increase in demand for factors of production may mean higher borrowing costs (financial crowding out) and higher wage costs for the private sector.
- May be inflationary - an increase in government spending pushes AD to the right increasing inflation.

Evaluation

- Higher national debt may only be cyclical rather than structural - may be due to recession, rather than an underlying problem. When there is a recovery in the economy it could go down again.
- Interest rates on gilts are very low at the moment, so this is less of a problem, and you could argue it's the right time to borrow.
- Unlikely to be inflationary at the moment as growth is slow and business and consumer confidence low.
- Sometimes government borrowing and spending is necessary to keep the economy afloat. Could argue this is one of those moments.

13.4 Ways of reducing a budget deficit

(a) Fiscal policies

(i) Increase taxation, e.g. income tax, corporation tax, VAT

The aim would be to increase tax revenues to reduce the deficit.

Evaluation

- It could disincentivise the workforce and affect productivity.
- It could affect entrepreneurship and innovation.
- May just increase tax evasion and avoidance so tax revenues don't really increase
- It may mean falling GDP in the future and therefore tax revenues would fall in the future as well.
- May deter foreign investment (FDI) and so effect jobs and growth.

(ii) Reduce government spending, e.g. on benefits, health and education

The aim would be to reduce government spending to reduce the deficit.

Evaluation

- Cutbacks in health and education could affect productivity and the long-term competitiveness of the economy.
- Reducing benefits would widen gaps between rich and poor.

(b) Monetary policy – decrease interest rates

This would increase consumption and create a multiplier effect. It would also encourage business investment. The net result should be that the economy grows and tax receipts rise and transfer payments fall.

Evaluation

- Might create inflation – therefore it works in the short run but makes the situation worse in the long run.

- Could cause the exchange rate to fall and create imported inflation
- Might create house price inflation

(c) Supply side policies

(i) Cut benefits

This would reduce government spending and create an incentive to work. Therefore, less people would claim benefit and those people would also become taxpayers increasing tax revenues.

Evaluation

- Could widen gaps between rich and poor
- Workers need to have jobs to go to
- May de-motivate the unemployed

(ii) Cut taxes e.g. income tax, corporation tax

This would create an incentive to work and gets people off benefits. It would also create an incentive for businesses to invest and expand creating more jobs. The net result would be that tax revenues rise and benefit payments fall reducing the deficit.

Evaluation

- Could widen gaps between rich and poor
- Workers need to have jobs to go to
- Corporation tax cuts might not be re-invested. They could just be spent on increased dividend payments or bonuses for directors.

(iii) Education and training

This would get people off benefits and into work therefore reducing the deficit.

Evaluation

- May have to raise taxes to pay for it
- Workers need to have jobs to go to
- Time lag

- Quality of courses

Productivity

14

14.1 Definition

Productivity measures the efficiency with which resources are used. The most commonly used productivity measure is labour productivity, which means output per worker. The two measures commonly used are GDP per worker and GDP per worker hour.

Productivity can also be measured by productivity of capital. Here the measure is output per unit of capital employed.

14.2 Factors effecting productivity

Just think about the factors of production. All the factors below are linked to them.

Investment - the more capital is substituted for labour the more output per worker will rise.
Education and training - if the skills of the workforce can be improved they will be able to do more complicated jobs with a higher value output. They will also produce more per worker.
Incentives to work more productively - if these can be increased workers will be more productive, e.g. taxes and benefits
Rules and regulations - these can hinder competition and make businesses more inefficient, e.g. employment regulations making it difficult to hire and fire workers.
Industrial unrest - strikes by unions and industrial unrest reduce productivity because it means less total output.

14.3 Importance

Productivity is important because it effects nearly all the governments' economic objectives:

Economic growth - lower output per worker means that GDP will fall so this slows down growth and will have an impact on living standards.
Unemployment - a productivity gap (see 14.5) with other countries implies loss of international competitiveness and a loss

of jobs. If output per worker is lower than other countries then labour costs per unit will be higher. This in turn has a knock-on effect to prices and competitiveness.

Inflation - high productivity keeps labour costs per unit low and inflation low. It means firms can compete harder on price and this is good for consumers.

Real incomes - if workers become more productive firms can afford to pay them higher wages. So productivity effects incomes.

Balance of payments - falling productivity will effect UK firms ability to compete in export markets abroad and against cheap imports at home. As stated previously, productivity effects labour costs per unit and therefore has a crucial effect on total costs per unit and competitiveness.

Evaluation

The effect of any productivity gap on the UK economy depends on a lot of different factors:

- Size of the productivity gap - it may just be small
- PED for exports and imports - if the PED for exports is inelastic the effect on exports and jobs may not be that large. Quality and branding may be more important than price.
- Exchange rate - if the exchange rate is falling it could cancel out any increase in costs
- Time lag

14.4 Policies to improve productivity

Mostly these are supply-side policies because they effect incentives to work more productively and incentives to invest. However, it also includes fiscal policies. Some suggestions are below:

(i) Cuts in income tax

- Should increase motivation at work, so workers work harder and create more output per head.
- Adds to the incentive to find a better paid more productive job.
- Cuts in the higher rate increase the incentive for people at the top to work harder, which then improves

management quality and productivity below them.
- Increases incentive to do overtime
- Increases incentive to seek promotion, so workers become more productive

Evaluation

- May increase gaps between rich and poor
- Needs to be a significant cut to effect motivation
- Just because you reduce tax doesn't necessarily mean people work harder
- May reduce tax revenues

(ii) Cuts in corporation tax

- Increases profitability so firms can spend more on investment
- Creates incentive to expand and be more competitive

Evaluation

- Higher profits may just mean bigger dividends for shareholders
- Extra profits may just be spent on bigger bonuses for directors, managers

(iii) Cuts in benefit, e.g. JSA, working family tax credit

- Creates incentive for people at work to be more productive to keep their jobs
- Cuts in in-work benefits raise incentive for workers to be do more hours and be more productive

Evaluation

- May increase gaps between rich and poor

(iv) Training and education

- Improves skills of the workforce so they can do higher paying more productive jobs
- Fills skills gaps so firms become more productive

Evaluation

- Cost - may have to raise taxes to pay for it
- Time lag - it may take 2/3 years or longer to work. It takes 7 years to go through secondary education
- Quality - expansion of higher education has been criticised as not being vocational enough by employers.

(v) Others

- Improvements in infrastructure, e.g. rail, roads, internet
- Increased spending on healthcare/NHS
- Increased immigration to fill skill shortages and provide competition in the labour market
- Deregulation of markets to create stronger competition and promote efficiency

14.5 Productivity gap

This means the difference in productivity from one country to another. For many years UK productivity has lagged behind that of Germany, France and the USA, and economists have put this down to various factors such as lower investment, skills of the workforce and incentives (see 14.2).

Relative merits of supply-side and demand-side policies as a means of realising policy objectives

15

15.1 Supply-side policies

(i) Unemployment

Policies

- Tax cuts, e.g. income tax, corporation tax
- Training and education
- Reduce benefits

Mechanism

- Tax cuts – income tax cuts create incentive to work, corporation tax cuts create incentive to invest and expand creating jobs.
- Reduce benefits – create incentive to work.
- Training and education – give unemployed the skills to find a job.

Evaluation

- Tax cuts – income tax cuts could widen gaps between rich and the poor, corporation tax cuts may just mean bigger dividends for shareholders.
- Reduce benefits - widens gaps between rich and the poor.
- Training and education – time lags and quality.

(ii) Inflation

Policies

- Increase flexibility of labour markets, e.g. trade union reform, reduce benefits, training and education
- Privatisation and deregulation

Mechanism

- Increased flexibility in the labour market puts downward pressure on wages which reduces firm's costs – therefore prices won't rise as much.
- Privatisation and deregulation increases competition.

Evaluation

- Increase flexibility of the labour market – unpopular with voters, therefore may be difficult to implement.
- Privatisation and deregulation – most of this has now been done; there's not much left to privatise.

(iii) Economic growth

Policies

- Tax cuts, e.g. income tax and corporation tax
- Privatisation
- Training and education
- Reduce benefits

Mechanism

- Tax cuts – income tax cuts create an incentive to work, corporation tax cuts create an incentive to start your own business. Income tax cuts also increase consumption.
- Privatisation – reduces waste and promotes efficiency in public services.
- Training and education – equips workers with the right skills and ensures the long-term competitiveness of the economy.
- Reduce benefits – creates an incentive to work and reduces unemployment.

Evaluation

- Tax cuts - income tax cuts could widen gaps between rich and the poor
- Reduce benefits – widens gaps between rich and the poor.
- Privatisation – not much left to do.
- Training and education – time lag and quality.

(iv) Redistribution of income

Policies

- Tax cuts, e.g. income tax
- Reduce benefits
- Training and education

Mechanism

- Tax cuts – income tax cuts create an incentive to work, salaries are higher than benefits therefore it reduces income inequalities.
- Reduce benefits - creates an incentive to work, salaries are higher than benefits therefore income inequalities reduce.
- Training and education – equips workers with the right skills, therefore they can get a job.

Evaluation

- Tax cuts – income tax cuts could widen income differentials.
- Reduce benefits - widens income differentials.
- Training and education – time lag and quality.

(v) Balance of payments

Policies

- Tax cuts, e.g. income tax, corporation tax
- Reduce benefits
- Training and education

Mechanism

- Tax cuts – income tax cuts improve motivation at work and increases productivity, corporation tax cuts mean more investment therefore competitiveness of UK businesses improves.
- Reduce benefits – creates an incentive to work and improves productivity.

66

- Training and education – improves the skill of the workforce.

Evaluation

- Tax cuts – income tax cuts could widen income differentials, corporation tax cuts may just mean bigger dividends for shareholders not more investment.
- Reduce benefits - widens income differentials.
- Training and education – time lags and quality.

15.2 Fiscal policy

(i) Unemployment

Policies

- Reduce taxes, e.g. income tax
- Increase government spending

Mechanism

- Reduce taxes – cuts in income tax increase disposable income, therefore consumption increases and creates a multiplier effect across the economy which creates more jobs.
- Increase government spending, e.g. health, education, transport. Creates more jobs on public sector projects and in public services, also creates a multiplier effect.

Evaluation

- Reduce taxes – tax cuts might be saved not spent.
- Increase government spending – could be wasted and might have to raise taxes to pay for it, therefore it could affect incentives.

(ii) Inflation

Policies

- Increase taxes, e.g. income tax
- Reduce government spending

Mechanism

- Increase taxes – reduces disposable income. Therefore reduces consumer spending and slows down price increases.
- Reduce government spending – shifts aggregate demand to the left and slows down price increases.

Evaluation

- Increase taxes – effects incentives to work. Therefore effects productivity and long run competitiveness of the economy.
- Reduce government spending – might mean public services deteriorate in the long run, e.g. health, education.

(iii) Economic growth

Policies

- Reduce taxes, e.g. income tax, corporation tax
- Increase government spending

Mechanism

- Reduce taxes – cuts in income tax should increase consumption shifting AD to the right. Cuts in corporation tax should increase investment and have the same effect.
- Increase government spending – improves public services and infrastructure, e.g. health, education, transport and therefore in the long run improves the competitiveness of the UK economy. Also shifts AD to the right.

Evaluation

- Reduce taxes – cuts in income tax could be saved not spent and might widen income differentials; cuts in corporation tax might just mean bigger dividends for shareholders.
- Increase government spending – might create inflation.

(iv) Redistribution of income

Policies

- Increase taxes
- Increase government spending

Mechanism

- Increase taxes – can afford to spend more on education, health and benefits.
- Increase government spending – on education, health and benefits.

Evaluation

- Increase taxes – effects incentives to work and productivity.
- May just result in more tax evasion (illegal) and tax avoidance (legal) so doesn't increase tax revenue.
- Increase government spending – spending on education may mean it just gets wasted on non-vocational courses. Increased spending on benefits may disincentivise getting a job.

(v) Balance of payments

Policies

- Increase taxes, e.g. income tax
- Export subsidies
- Import controls, e.g. tariffs.

Mechanism

- Increase taxes – increase in income tax reduces disposable income. This reduces spending on all goods including imports and corrects a balance of payment deficit.
- Export subsidies – creates incentive to export.
- Import tariffs and quota restrictions – makes it harder for imports to come into the country.

Evaluation

- increase taxes – slows down spending so might trigger off a recession.
- Export subsidies – retaliation, might lead to long-term contraction in trade.
- Import controls – as for export subsidies.

15.3 Monetary policy

(i) Unemployment

Policies

- Reduce interest rates

Mechanism

- Increases disposable income because mortgages get cheaper – therefore increases consumption and creates more jobs.
- Makes business investment cheaper, so encourages firms to expand

Evaluation

- Consumer confidence and business confidence may be low, so doesn't really increase consumption or investment.
- Might create house price inflation because it makes mortgages cheaper.
- Might create too much consumption – therefore creates inflation.
- Time lag
- Reduced mortgage payments might be saved not spent

(ii) Inflation

Policies

- Raise interest rate

Mechanism

- Reduces disposable income – therefore decreases consumption and shifts AD to the left.

Evaluation

- Raise interest rate - raises exchange rate, therefore exports get more expensive and balance of payments deteriorates.
- Time lag

(iii) Economic growth

Policies

- Reduce interest rate

Mechanism

- Increases consumption and shifts AD to the right.
- Makes it cheaper for businesses to borrow money to invest – therefore increases productivity and shifts AS to the right.

Evaluation

- Might create inflation.
- Might mean the exchange rate falls and therefore imports get more expensive creating 'imported inflation'.
- Time lag
- Might create house price inflation because it becomes cheaper to get a mortgage – therefore personal debt grows.
- Consumer confidence and business confidence may be low, so doesn't really increase consumption or investment.
- Reduced mortgage payments might be saved not spent

(iv) Redistribution of income

Policies

- Reduce interest rate

Mechanism

- Increases disposable income and therefore creates more consumption – this creates a multiplier effect and more jobs.
- Makes it cheaper for businesses to borrow money and invest and therefore productivity and competitiveness improves creating more jobs.

Evaluation

- Knock on effect to house prices - could create house price inflation.
- Knock on effect to imports – could mean the exchange rate falls and creates 'imported inflation'.
- Time lag

(v) Balance of payments

Policies

- Reduce interest rate

Mechanism

- Should mean the exchange rate falls and therefore exports get cheaper and imports more expensive improving the balance of payments.
- Makes business investment cheaper. Therefore raises productivity, reduces costs and makes it easier for businesses to export.

Evaluation

- Knock-on effect to spending – might create inflation because borrowing is cheaper.
- Knock-on effect to housing market - might create house price inflation because lower interest rates means mortgages are cheaper.
- Time lag

The Phillips curve

16

The Phillips curve shows there is an inverse relationship between inflation and unemployment. As unemployment rises inflation falls and as unemployment falls inflation rises. We can explain this two ways:

(1) **Demand-pull inflation** – as unemployment falls consumption rises pushing AD to the right. This raises the price level increasing inflation. Similarly, if unemployment rises consumption will fall causing a fall in inflation.

(2) **Cost-push inflation** – as unemployment rises workers realise they are in a weak position to bargain up wages and so keep pay claims down. This means production costs will fall and firms can keep prices down causing a fall in inflation. Similarly, if unemployment fell workers would realise there is stronger competition for their labour so they could bargain up wages causing firms costs to rise and so inflation to rise.

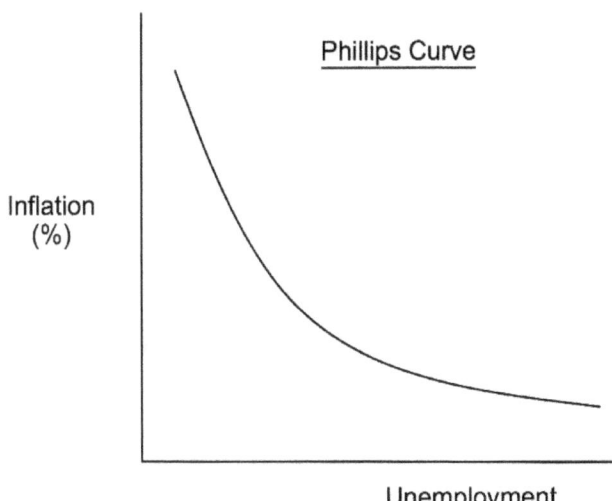

Phillips Curve

Inflation (%)

Unemployment

Conflicts between government economic objectives

17

17.1 Government economic objectives

Remember these are:

- Full employment
- Price stability
- Economic growth
- Balance of payments equilibrium
- Income redistribution
- Balanced government budget
- Care for the environment

17.2 Conflicts between objectives

There are many ways in which the government's economic objectives can conflict with each other. Below are some of the best examples:

(i) Economic growth vs. inflation

Rapid growth can lead to shortages of raw materials and labour. This increases costs and causes cost-push inflation. If there is excess demand in the economy it will cause demand pull inflation as well.

(ii) Economic growth vs. full employment

Rapid growth can lead to technological and structural unemployment. People who used to work in the "old economy" can't be retrained quickly enough to work in the "new economy".

(iii) Economic growth vs. balance of payments

Economic growth can lead to balance of payments problems if domestic producers can't keep pace with demand and goods and raw materials have to be imported from abroad.

(iv) Economic growth vs. redistribution of income

Economic growth can lead to increasing gaps between rich and poor if it's not managed properly by the government. They need to make careful use of the tax and benefit system to make sure this doesn't happen.

(v) Economic growth vs. externalities

Economic growth can cause an increase in external costs like pollution, congestion and greenhouse gases. This can become an economic cost, which is a burden to future generations.

(vi) Full employment vs. low inflation

Phillips curve analysis predicts that if we want to have full employment then this will cause high inflation, and if we want to have low inflation we need to have high unemployment. To have both at the same time doesn't seem possible - although it's true this seems to be contradicted today.

(vii) Full employment vs. balance of payments

Full employment is usually associated with rising real incomes and rising spending. This can lead to balance of payments problems if domestic producers can't satisfy demand and goods and raw materials have to be imported from abroad instead.

Index

W

wealth, 43, 44

wealth effect, 22, 35, 38, 48
withdrawals, 19